Kiss & Tell

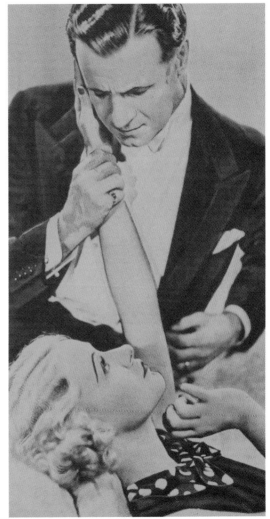

Kiss and Tell

BROWN DOG BOOKS

4

The Art of Romance

I just met a wonderful new man. He's fictional…but you can't have everything.

Mia Farrow as Celia
***Purple Rose of Cairo*, 1985**

Love is too weak a word for what I feel – I luuurve you, you know, I loave you, I luff you.

Alvy Singer (Woody Allen) to Annie Hall (Diane Keaton)
***Annie Hall*, 1977**

Carol: You kissed me and I was thrilled.

Jerry: A kiss? What does that prove? It's like finding out you can light a stove. It doesn't make you a cook.

Doris Day and Rock Hudson
Lover Come Back, 1961

I'm a happily married woman
– or, rather, I was until a few weeks ago.

This is my whole world, and it's enough
– or, rather, it was until a few weeks ago.

But, oh, Fred, I've been so foolish.

I've fallen in love.

I'm an ordinary woman. I didn't think
such violent things could happen to
ordinary people.

Celia Johnson as Laura
Brief Encounter, 1946

Romances that began on set

Humphrey Bogart & Lauren Bacall
To Have and Have Not, 1944

Barbara Streisand & Omar Sharif
Funny Girl, 1968

William Hurt & Marlee Matlin
Children of a Lesser God, 1986

John Malkovich & Michelle Pfeiffer
Dangerous Liaisons, 1988

Meg Ryan & Russell Crowe
Proof of Life, 2000

Brad Pitt & Gwyneth Paltrow
Seven, 1995

Burt Reynolds & Sally Field
Smokey and the Bandit, 1977

Steve McQueen & Ali McGraw
The Getaway, 1972

Jeff Goldblum & Laura Dern
Jurassic Park, 1993

Gabriel Bryne & Ellen Barkin
Siesta, 1987

I enjoy and so believe
in love, what would
I do without it?

Nicole Kidman as Satine
Moulin Rouge, 2000

C'est tellement simple, l'amour.

Arletty as Garance
Les Enfants du Paradis, 1945

Love, I love beyond breath, beyond reason, beyond love's own power of loving!

Gerard Depardieu
Cyrano de Bergerac, 1990

How can one change one's entire life and build a new one on one moment of love? And yet, that's what you make me want to close my eyes and do.

**Marguerite (Greta Garbo)
to Armand (Robert Taylor)**
Camille, 1936

More romances that began on set

Mickey Rourke & Carrie Otis
Wild Orchid, 1990

Ryan O'Neal & Ali McGraw
Love Story, 1970

Susan Sarandon & Tim Robbins
Bull Durham, 1988

Tom Cruise & Nicole Kidman
Far and Away, 1992

Julia Roberts & Lyle Lovett
The Player, 1992

Warren Beatty & Annette Bening
Bugsy, 1991

Jessica Lange & Sam Shepard
Frances, 1982

Madonna & Sean Penn
Shanghai Surprise, 1986

Clint Eastwood & Jean Seberg
Paint Your Wagon, 1969

Clark Gable & Loretta Young
The Call of the Wild, 1935

You must allow me to tell you how ardently I admire and love you.

Colin Firth as Mr. Darcy
Pride and Prejudice, 1995

Yer beautiful in yer wrath! I shall keep you, and in responding to my passions, yer hatred will kindle into love.

John Wayne as Genghis Kahn
The Conqueror, 1956

Not only did I enjoy that kiss last night,
I was awed by the efficiency behind it.

John (Cary Grant) to Frances (Grace Kelly)
To Catch a Thief, 1955

Kisses

When Clark Gable kissed me, they had to carry me off the set.

Carroll Baker

But I wasn't kissing her, I was whispering in her mouth.

Chico Marx (when his wife caught him kissing a chorus girl)

I've been kissing Audrey Hepburn all day and my pucker is tuckered.

James Garner

A kiss is a lovely trick designed by nature to stop speech when words become superfluous.

Ingrid Bergman

The Art of Seduction

I have this thing about saxophone players, especially tenor sax… I don't know what it is, but they just curdle me. All they have to do is play eight bars of 'Come to Me, My Melancholy Baby' and my spine turns to custard. I get goose pimply all over and I come to 'em.

Marilyn Monroe as Sugar
Some Like It Hot, 1959

Ben: Mrs Robinson, you're trying to seduce me. Aren't you?

Mrs Robinson: Would you like me to seduce you? Is that what you want?

Dustin Hoffman and Anne Bancroft
The Graduate, 1967

I know how you feel. You don't know if you want to hit me or kiss me. I get a lot of that.

Madonna as Mahoney
Dick Tracey, 1990

Gee, Dennis, I don't want any ceremony but turn around and give me the works.

Jean Harlow as Vantine (asking Clark Gable for a goodnight kiss)
Red Dust, 1932

Now I am going to take you in my arms and kiss you very quickly and very hard.

Richard (Tom Ewell) to The Girl (Marilyn Monroe)
The Seven Year Itch, 1955

You should be kissed and often and by someone who knows how.

Rhett (Clark Gable) to Scarlet (Vivien Leigh)
Gone with the Wind, 1939

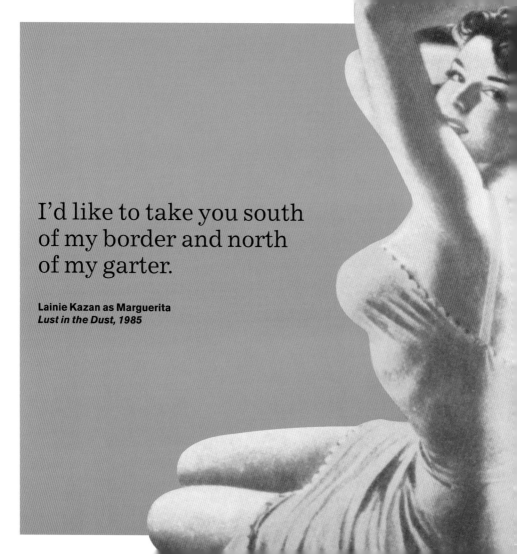

I'd like to take you south of my border and north of my garter.

Lainie Kazan as Marguerita
Lust in the Dust, 1985

Anytime you got nuthin' to do and lots o' time to do it, come up!

Mae West as Flower Belle Lee
My Little Chickadee, 1940

Ten Most Passionate Movies

Gone with the Wind, 1939
Clark Gable & Vivien Leigh

To Have and Have Not, 1944
Humphrey Bogart & Lauren Bacall

The Postman Always Rings Twice, 1945
Lana Turner & Robert Taylor

Notorious, 1946
Cary Grant & Ingrid Bergman

From Here to Eternity, 1953
Burt Lancaster & Deborah Kerr

Breathless, 1960
Jean-Paul Belmondo & Jean Sebert

The Thomas Crown Affair, 1968
Steve McQueen & Faye Dunaway

Body Heat, 1981
Kathleen Turner & William Hurt

Basic Instinct, 1992
Sharon Stone & Michael Douglas

The English Patient, 1996
Ralph Fiennes & Kristin Scott Thomas

I appreciate this whole seduction thing you've got going on but let me give you a tip:

I'm a sure thing.

Julia Roberts as Vivian
Pretty Woman, 1991

You know, you don't have to act with me, Steve. You don't have to say anything, and you don't have to do anything. Not a thing.

Oh, maybe just a whistle. You know how to whistle, don't you Steve? You just put your lips together and blow.

Slim (Lauren Bacall) to Steve (Humphrey Bogart)
To Have and Have Not, 1944

Sex Appeal

I like to be naked in movies, I've a reputation to uphold.

Alec Baldwin

If a woman thinks she's sexy, she is.

Burt Reynolds

Nudity is easier if there are two of you.

Greta Scacchi

I may not be the greatest actress but I've become the greatest at screen orgasms. Ten seconds of heavy breathing, roll your head from side to side, simulate a slight asthma attack, and die a little.

Candice Bergen

Flo: Hold me closer, closer, closer.

Dr. Hackenbush: If I hold you any closer, I'll be in back of you.

Esther Muir and Groucho Marx
A Day at the Races, 1937

Baby, you're the key to my ignition.

**Helen (Charlotte Greenwood)
to Eddie (Eddie Cantor)**
Palmy Days, 1931

Listen, Sweetheart, you shouldn't listen to what a woman says when she's in the throes of passion. They say the darndest things.

Susan Sarandon as Annie
Bull Durham, 1988

Together Forever

All I know is I had a good time last night. I'm going to have a good time tonight. If we have enough good times together, I'm going to get down on my knees. I'm going to beg that girl to marry me. If we make a party on New Year's, I got a date for that party. You don't like her? That's too bad.

Ernest Borgnine
Marty, 1955

No matter who you marry,
you wake up married to
someone else.

Marlon Brando as Sky
Guys and Dolls, 1955

Jerry: Osgood, I'm going to
level with you. We can't get
married at all…(removing
wig) I'm a man.
Osgood:
Well, nobody's perfect.

Jack Lemmon and E. Fielding III
Some Like It Hot, 1959

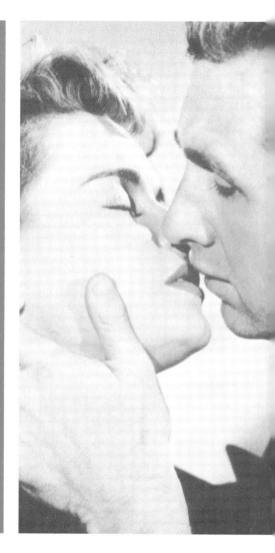

When I want to kiss my wife, I'll kiss her anytime, anyplace, anywhere. That's the kind of hairpin I am.

James Cagney as Biff
The Strawberry Blonde, 1941

I love that you get cold when it's 71 degrees out. I love that it takes you an hour and a half to order a sandwich. I love that you get a little crinkle in your nose when you're looking at me like I'm nuts…and I love that you are the last person I want to talk to before I go to sleep at night. And it's not because I'm lonely and it's not because it's New Year's Eve. I came here tonight because when you realize you want to spend the rest of your life with somebody, you want the rest of your life to start as soon as possible.

Billy Crystal to Meg Ryan
When Harry Met Sally, 1989

Lovers

Age does not protect you from love, but love to some extent protects you from age.

Jeanne Moreau

If love is blind, why is lingerie so popular?

Mickey Rooney

Love means never having to say you're sorry.

Erich Segal
(from Love Story)

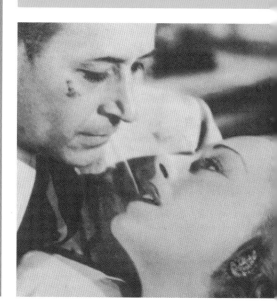

I don't remember how many lovers I've had. I was never interested in the score – only the game. I've been on more laps than a napkin.

Mae West

When you fall in love it is a temporary madness. It erupts like an earthquake and then it subsides. And when it subsides you have to work out whether your roots have become so entwined together it is inconceivable that you should ever part.

John Hurt as Iannis
Captain Corelli's Mandolin, 2001

Ten Romantic Movies

It Happened One Night, 1934
Clark Gable & Claudette Colbert

Casablanca, 1942
Humphrey Bogart & Ingrid Bergman

Brief Encounter, 1946
Trevor Howard & Celia Johnson

Dr. Zhivago, 1965
Julie Christie & Omar Sharif

A Man and A Woman, 1966
Anouk Aimee & Jean-Louis Trintignant

Love Story, 1970
Ali McGraw & Ryan O'Neal

Ghost, 1990
Demi Moore & Patrick Swayze

Sleepless in Seattle, 1993
Meg Ryan & Tom Hanks

Titanic, 1997
Kate Winslet & Leonardo di Caprio

Captain Corelli's Mandolin, 2001
Nicholas Cage & Penelope Cruz

Marriage

Our marriage works because we carry clubs of equal weight and size.

Paul Newman

If you want to sacrifice the admiration of many men, for the criticism of one, go ahead: get married.

Katherine Hepburn

In my house I'm the boss. My wife is just the decision-maker.

Woody Allen

Marriage is a great institution.

Elizabeth Taylor

Ten Romances that have stood the test of time

Laurence Olivier & Vivien Leigh
Jessica Lange & Sam Shepard
Mary Pickford & Douglas Fairbanks
Paul Newman & Joanne Woodward
Sarah Jessica Parker & Matthew Broderick
Susan Sarandon & Tim Robbins
Warren Beatty & Annette Bening
Jessica Tandy & Hume Cronin
Goldie Hawn & Kurt Russell
Ralph Fiennes & Francesca Annis

Published in 2006 in the United Kingdom by

Brown Dog Books
6 The Old Dairy
Melcombe Road
Bath
BA2 3LR

Brown Dog Books is an imprint of The Manning Partnership.
www.manning-partnership.co.uk

Conceived and produced by
Elwin Street Limited
79 St John St
London EC1M 4NR
www.elwinstreet.com

A CIP catalogue record for this book is available from the British Library

10-digit ISBN 1-90-305619-5
13-digit ISBN 978-1-903056-19-6

Designed by Esther Kirkpatrick

Printed in China

10 9 8 7 6 5 4 3 2 1